For Stephanie Burt

BLUE SANDBAR
MOON

With every good
wish—

chris Agee
23·IX· 2019
Harvard

About the Author

Chris Agee is a poet, essayist, photographer and editor. His third collection of poems, *Next to Nothing,* was shortlisted in Britain for the 2009 Ted Hughes Award for New Work in Poetry. He recently edited *Balkan Essays*, the sixth volume of Hubert Butler's essays. He lives in Belfast, and divides his time between Ireland, Scotland and Croatia.

BLUE SANDBAR MOON

A micro-epic

CHRIS AGEE

THE IRISH PAGES PRESS
2018

Blue Sandbar
Moon
is first published in hardback
on 1 November 2018.

The Irish Pages Press
129 Ormeau Road
Belfast BT7 1SH
Ireland

www.irishpages.org

Typeset in 12/15 pt Monotype Perpetua
Designed, composed and printed by Nicholson & Bass, Belfast

A CIP catalogue record for this book
is available from The British Library.

Dust-jacket photograph: Jacob Agee
Cover designs: Charles Gouldsbrough

ISBN: 978-0-9935532-1-9

Also by Chris Agee

POETRY

In the New Hampshire Woods
(1992)

First Light
(2003)

Next to Nothing
(2008)

AS EDITOR

Scar on the Stone: Contemporary Poetry from Bosnia
(1998)

Unfinished Ireland: Essays on Hubert Butler
(2003)

The New North: Contemporary Poetry from Northern Ireland
(2008)

*The Other Tongues: An Introduction to Irish, Scots Gaelic
and Scots in Ulster and Scotland*
(2013)

Balkan Essays
by Hubert Butler
(2016)

For the cherished ones, con amore

CONTENTS

PROEM

OPENINGS
A micro-epic

Proem

2007 – 2010

SUMMER PLUMS

In the valley before Srebrenica the corn was the tallest
I've ever seen. Someone was reaping by sickle
what looked like lavender. Another was scything silage.
Several places, women in kerchiefs and pantaloons
were sat on grass before their houses, looking out.
Low steep hills ringed the valley

with thick woods. There were domed Bosnian
haystacks pinnacled with poles and shells of ruined houses
colonized by undergrowth. It seemed right to return
to renew fields and gardens amid beckoning ghosts
of family and neighbours. A cow was led
on a rope by an old woman in the same dress

and a girl in shorts walked the road
to Potočari. A windfall of apples was
down in an orchard and silken plums scattered
on a forested lane. Two headstones stood
in a cornfield like a summer host
of thousands of splendid ears.

LIGHTSCAPE: AFTERMATH

All the hay's up high
like rusted memory
of Jugoslavia at heyday –
or was, cut here for summer.
Seeded in the heart's derelict eye

like a patch of old peasant ground
by a shed door bearing one board's
truncated red S L A V I A .
Or a quartermoon sickle at midday
vanishing like a ghostly helmet

through the blue afternoon.
Or Cavafy's moon of nocturnal desires
washed up on the foreshore of noon.
Or the same late Moon like
a beautiful amber peach-slice

descending through almond branches.
Or even a cumbersome Communist sideboard bespeaking
the final dismantling of that household ensemble
that was with you that first summer of aftermath.
Landscape, timescape, heartscape, lightscape –

who can say where
one begins, another ends,
or all conjoin, commingle
as if the world's every thing
was its own image for something else?

NERETVA RESTAURANT

I'd forgotten that half-an-hour-or-so
until a few days before our bus swung in again
to the sloping roadside restaurant
perched on an overlook high above
the dazzling Neretva threaded below
the white conical minarets and strip fields, the Yugoslav pylons

of beautiful Jablanica. A pumped and cobblestoned rill
was bubbling from top to bottom, through a series
of gutters, waterwheels, pipes and cement fish-tanks
where trout were penned in dappled beauty.
Eight lamb-spits filled the air with woodsmoke and its smell.
I remember a quick lunch and nothing of Miriam

but love and presence. At the back, in the woods
below the dining deck, a breath of presence,
ash-flicker and mapleleaf flutter
in the high heat of Central Europe.
I stood perspirant with Jacob and watched far below
a brown, pebbled, submarine sandbar

like a trout's speckled belly
in the crook of a wooded bend –
depths turquoise, shallows green,
under another day's
dazzling
blue river.

in memory of Miriam

AFTER RAINS

A large seed-parachute from a plant's pod
floated up from the night yard
and rose into the door's lampshine
on fresh air's slightest breath
like thistledown in slow motion,
a snow-crystal, or some sea creature
out of the abysmal depths. I knew before I tried

I would never find it.
It was so linty and delicate, so immaterial,
it would vanish as spider's web
on the wet Earth's solidities.
It reminded me instantly of that first May
thistledown after apocalypse.
When I moved forward, it moved off and down

towards the dark beyond the table legs.
When I searched the verandah flagstones, half-lit
in penumbra, it was nowhere
to be found. When I shone a flashlight
close-up on the stone, there was still no trace
of its image, a trout-fly reeled in.
Some low undercurrent

probably took it from my ken.
It felt like a last omen,
approached and touched me,
and returned to the night.

MOONRISE, NEW YEAR'S EVE

The moon rose behind us.
We turned to face

its full large dial
low over Bloody Foreland.

It cast its wavering
phenomenological foil over

the bay's whale-road and seal-road.
A wisp of cloud

twisted a half-veil
over its shadowy

seas. A scudding bank
first topped it

like a matador's hat,
then blocked it

with a backlit darkness.
Spindrift's suds

fled the rising tideline
in a tumbleweed

of moments
whitening the night.

Glad your old Dad's
still here? Give me a kiss.

It's good being
together, huh?

That was always, of
course, the real reason

for our time
in Donegal.

SNOW IN DUBLIN: EPIPHANY

The snow
one always knew

but had never seen
save in

the background scene
of the Joycean *Dead*

was muffling down
in Merrion Square,

St Stephen's Green,
doe-eyed flakes

in the plateglass
of the O2

shop on Grafton Street
after that gallivant

across Ireland
on the *Enterprise*

when I found propped miraculously
on a snowy railing

the glasses case
I had dropped

in the daily slush.
In a snow-laden atrium

in the Liberties
the world was transformed –

I felt it in myself,
drifting and drifting.

How had
I got this far,

to the unconditional,
the irreplaceable

hinging optatively
on a flickering *Departures* board?

Beautiful heart-manna
of snowy Dublin,

like a fine Jewish linen,
muslin or damask ...

covering now,
time enough,

the old world
of my defeated days.

PARABLE OF A SUMMER

Another call, email, task, list, purchase, repair, reconstruction, focus, meeting, movement. Another *thing*. Above all, in all this – covering all this – another thing-to-do. What might it mean, in an ontological sense? It is, I'd say, Roth's "dream of endlessness" – the assumption, on some primordial psychological level, owing to each past day's renewal of *presence* present, that we will never end. At some point, it all seems to say, we will reach the paradisiacal terminus of completion, the plenitude, or platitude, of *everything done*.

But for most of us, I daresay, looking back, it will never have happened. Paradise not lost, but unmaterialized. More of an Elysium of shadowy tasks in the foreground of missed existence. More *Microsoft Office* than the *Word* of life's real presence. Sisyphus in the half-life of his daily incline, daily decline.

Up above us, like some caul of techno-bioluminescence we've lately developed, the jellyfish of new communication floats in the ether of near space, moored to its satellites. It is clear that a large proportion of humanity, already, cannot elude it for more than a few days, or contemplate living without it.

———

Birdwatching is subtle. One of the eye's subtle arts. An art, too, of the ear. And extremely ancient: the stuff of augury and omen. It is strange to think that these creatures might be the shrunken dwarves of pterodactyls and dinosaural colour.

You can see, though, why many will see nothing in it. Its narrow visual range, its endless repetitions.

A few swallows pirouetting like jets through the morning yard – their blue-black backs, their white bellies. The secretive flash of the golden oriole. An owl taking wing out of the almonds against the last light of the valley. Flocks of little brown birds, unidentified, seeking gleanings at raked dawn on our old gravelly road between parched grasses, disturbed into flight by an opened door. The strange grace of the house bats tumbling headlong through the same yard as soon as dark falls. Up from Africa in April, the hoarse serenade of nightingales, trilling and squeaking in the crisp and starry night. Could there really be much in it?

But it teaches you to attend. To wait on the small thing and the little surprise. To abandon the pseudo-cosmic disease for the narrower reaches of a microcosmos. To plumb intently, as with augury or Newton, just one moment's becoming on the ground of physical being. Where that small surprise can take wing into the imaginations of one's full attention.

And on almost every occasion of such attention, there are surprises. Like one time when a small bird with rufous back, buff belly and black mask alighted in sunshine on the almond sapling in front of the terrace. The species is common, if still unidentified; but I had never quite noticed the marvel of its glossy back, its rufous sheen.

Till that minute on the morning in question. I might not have stepped one leg up on the wall of the terrace and looked in that direction. I might have been thinking of emails.

Updike has spoken of the increasing "dephysicalization" of contemporary culture. Is this, then, now the one globalized, dominant ontology-ideology? If so, in this sense, for me in any event, a rufous gloss must always trump – or out-Trump – any email.

———◆———

People in the village are always giving each other little gifts. It is a kind of barter of goodwill and neighbourly feeling.

One morning I saw an old neighbour's wife meet Jasinka, a younger neighbour, on the crumbling tarmac that runs by our house through weathered stone walls. The Žrnovo church clock was just striking its nine chimes. After the loud and public greetings that are typical, she immediately gave Jasinka a plastic bag of tomatoes from her garden. Whether the tomatoes were intended for Jasinka, or whether they were to be unloaded on the first friend or neighbour she encountered on the road, was unclear. It always is . . .

Another morning, our neighbour Petar, who seldom visits, suddenly appeared round the corner of the house from the tarmac lane. The terrace was still in shade and I was taking an early breakfast alone. He was shirtless and in sandals, with a straw hat like Huck Finn's. He brought me a bag of two cucumbers and four tomatoes, of the heartshaped local variety, always very good. Perhaps it was also an occasion to remark on my three haystacks: that after my last misjudgement with petrol in May, scorching the cypress, they should not be burnt until October. The island's summer tinderbox of scrub forest, parched vegetation and grassy olive groves was a perennial threat.

His gift lifted my spirits at the start of another hot day. It was like a cool mental dew in the optimism of the morning. Its common quality, over time, across village space, partly informs, and partly inspired, this prose.

———•———

A black ant scampers across the creamy white of a limestone jamb.

Dalmatian light and dark.

Everything – *every thing* – is interesting.

Later, not far from the stone threshold, another ant – or, maybe, the same one – hauls its awn of straw, with Sisyphean purpose, towards the Eocene's version of our own technohive.

Žrnovo, Croatia
Summer 2007

A micro-epic

2008-2017

2008-2009

"... My imagination
is a piece of board
my sole instrument
is a wooden stick ..."

Zbigniew Herbert
from "A Knocker"

I made it

on time
this year
defeated
and tired
your scent still
with me
thin and delicate
in the drafts
of hindsight

Belfast
May 2008

Is it

possible
to be returning
all your life
to a Penelope
you've
never met

Belfast
April 2009

Facing

my fate
I walk
to the shop
to collect
the review
through shadowy
magnolia
blossoms
under
the brilliant
blue
the low sun
behind
warming
my living
neck

Belfast
11 April 2009

New leaf

in the shaggy
birches
dewy daffodil
and the weeping
willow
buds bursting
everywhere
in the wan sunshine
the same
weak scent
fading
at the second take
choked up
inside

Belfast
17 April 2009

Deathly pale

Girl from the Van Valkenburg Family
on her Deathbed

brightly live

Still Life
with Wild Strawberries
and one white
flower

Mauritshuis
The Hague
23 April 2009

Rembrandt

the human face
the central light
the inner glow

the

Mauritshuis
The Hague
23 April 2009

IN THE HAGUE

Late bright

sunshine
the fountain's
recycled Calder
the Court
breaks
universe of pain
the screening
at Potočari
in
evidential rules
I discern
your small act
of unkindness

At the Tribunal

prosecutors
in pearls

in the Mauritshuis
Girl
with a Pearl
Earring
her lips open
turning
to face you

each thing
so
so human

Blown along

the bike-track
drifts of fluttering
heart-shaped beige catkins
like legions
of the lost
thronging
and imploring
the gates
of the living
Tribunal

International Criminal Tribunal
  for the Former Yugoslavia
The Hague
May 2009

Reality's light

clear and hard
bright healthy
yourself in
aftermath
one day
at a time
giving the day
its due

After Delft
The Hague
4 May 2009

Flat fields

from the train
the canals
lucent
a march of poplars
and I sleep
for a second
a moment's blink
and I wake
to the lost
you again
the depth
under the Vermeer
veneer
of the every thing
feeling

Remembering Miriam
Zuid Holland
8 May 2009

Sun-gold

dark navy
Aphrodite's
churning sea-foam
and the ochre
cliffs above
mirrored deep
like fluid holograms
or isobars
in the wavering
depths
where consciousness
swims
in feeling

Dingli Cliffs
Malta
10 May 2009

The last

poem of the last
reading
of the festival
came in
marvellous winnowed Irish
rendered
roughly thus:

Here we go, trying
to separate
the infinite possibilities of life
from the limited circumstances
we prefer

At the last breath
none of us know
whether it was
the chaff or
the grain
that flew off in the wind

an epitaph
a sort
of willing tragedy
really

Remembering Holland
Valletta, Malta
11 May 2009

2010

"Being that can be understood is language."

Hans-Georg Gadamer

On the beach

inner Dunkirk

archery
only gets you so far

the pinprick
of Venus

is much
more important

Ireland
Late January, 2010

A petal

falling
from the magnolia
in the morning's
dusky gustiness
threatening
the tones
of another storm

Belfast
Spring 2010

Sweet scent

of magnolia
another
spring in
Central Park
first forsythia
the floating
locks of weeping
willows
two towers
of the Dakotas
and ice-rink and
soundtrack
in sunshine
bringing still
life's
perfect thing

New York City
Late March, 2010

Nine years

ago
today
your sister
was deathly ill
now
by chance
or happenstance
in St Paul's
under the lantern
and golden gallery
readings and addresses
a string quartet

silence is kept

giving way
or given away
when the cock crows
to the crowds
on this good Friday

"Silence is kept": from the Liturgy
St Paul's Cathedral, London
Good Friday, April 2010

Out of the dark

the crowds
thronging
the ramp
moment
of liberation
as if
from some Kosova-catastrophe
or
the barbed-wire
allées at Auschwitz

Then in

the dark a black sky
or black milk
the kids
screaming and running
velveteen walls
so turning

And turned

Rothko's gloaming-light like
a rose window
of all the daily
life
returning
ahead

Just a black box

man-made
steel structure
echoing the Turbine Hall's
the Dynamo's
how it is

Installation, Turbine Hall
Tate Modern, London
Good Friday, April 2010

Maybe

nothing today
as I will walk
past the place
where I held your hand
on the curbside
towards
the little window
where your bright face
bid me goodbye
every day
one magpie
pecking the grass
foaming sea-surf
of the memorial
magnolia
kids in the daffodils
the birds singing
again
and the eternal scent
for me
of your life
like the two blossoms
on the dining table
unfaded
as Chinese feeling
in the cut-crystal
bowl
of invisible waters

Anniversary of Miriam's deathday
Belfast
4 April 2010

By the fish house

foam
flecking the Corrib
from the frothing weirs
of the fathom-levels
leopardskin
skein or camouflage
netting
as if
leaves of light
were welling
moving and skeining
on or from
the deeps
purely
impenetrably
preternaturally
dark

Near the Fishery Tower
Galway
7 May 2010

Rams' horns

like spiral fossils
out of the Cretaceous
under Ben Bulben
and the sun
nibbling twixt
clumps of the Irish
rush
reeds fingering
the polished lough
screes and hill-skulls
afoam with gorse
flesher-flanks
the field-quilts drawn
by late light
the hedgerows fluttering
close
in the fresh airs
of Barry Cooke
or some chill
Yeatsian breeze
coursing
this perfect evening

Co Sligo
8 May 2010

All

at once
a bright coffin
in last light
in its hearse
all alone
and empty
on a rough lay-by
a cross
from the "Funeral House"
country removal cars
feathery hedges
log-piles and cattle-grates
the helium-orb
apocalypto
in red
flaming low
over the road
in my rear view
mirror

Near Belcoo
Co Fermanagh
8 May 2010

The clock

at Clogher
is time's
is art's
moon

in stone

The Protestant cathedral
Clogher, Co Tyrone
(Clogher: from the Irish, clochar,
"something made of stone")
8 May 2010

An old

working-class man
curtained off
in a cubicle
bullied by a doctor
off-hand
peremptory
authoritarian
on loan
from the Mater
he mentions
unclearly
the hospice
but is buoyed up
a bit
by the clipped 90 percent
of the next procedure
a rough
boyish face
unshaven
cheerio!
take care!
lucky me
having escaped again
I buy a pink German
biscuit
in memory of Miriam
tears in
the eyes
but *fuck your kind*
blunt brute Northerner
whom Joyce
hated too

Watching a doctor
City Hospital
11 May 2010

In

the Hugh Lane
10 Poets
Observe Silence
for sound depends
on silence
for
its form

Performance Piece
The Hugh Lane Gallery
21 May 2010

Just

like
the Angelus
the lama's
bronze bowl
is tapped
by the padded
Buddhic
baton

"Ten Poets Observe Silence"
The Hugh Lane Gallery
22 May 2010

Mná

Ladies

Fír
Men

is it
really
simply
the condition
of all
conditioning

A break
"Ten Poets Observe Silence"
22 May 2010

Looking through

the glass doors
the inside
already outside
in the blue-hearted
day

Seated in the Hugh Lane Gallery
22 May 2010

Afterwards

the London planes
dappling
five stone seats
now emptied

Parnell Square
Dublin
22 May 2010

Orange-golden

orb
low over
the Gasworks
in a gap
in the skyline
one carriage
glides in
another
slides out

Belfast Central Station
23 May 2010

Deep in

lush
Longford
the smell of slurry
birdsong and cows
and cow parsley
on stilled verges
old demesne
walls
ivied with ivy
I piss
through a rusted
curvilinear gate
towards countryscapes
under noctilucent
clouds
the canary
in the climate's
coalmine

Co Longford
5 June 2010

The white moonstone

in the late blue
at the lane's end
like a dot
on the chimneypot's

i

floating up
between
the frames
of the window-frame

North Parade
Belfast
July 2010

That's

my mother
a broken branch
held by a thread
after storms
browning high
on the great
round beech
under the breath of cumuli
and blues
of Mary's cloak

Ravenhill Road
Belfast
July 2010

No

darling
I won't
let go
no
it's all
I have
to keep
you here

Gortahork
Co Donegal
16 July 2010

The sun's blaze

at Koćje
glinting and
trickling
through the rustling
oaks
so cool
in the limestone dells
of pinnacles
so peaceful so beautiful
looking up
in the shadow
of the day's
atomic furnace

Koćje Nature Reserve
Korčula
Croatia
6 August 2010

Little white

ghost
you seem
so pale
and thin
and young
your two big eyes
and antennae
your body
a folded leaf
on legs
rocking in the wind
appearing
once again
on stone
small joy
of presence
in absence
as we work
cutting grass
and the old brambles

Praying mantis
Žrnovo
Croatia
7 August 2010

Amazing

green-grey eyes
a girl's
huge irises
in a woman's
body
on the boat
from Mljet
I remember
the day
we nicknamed
you
Wolf Eyes
radiant delphiniums
speckled
with yellow
on the same ferry
at the same
afternoon hour

Between Korčula and Mljet
August 2010

It was once

so bright
and shiny
new-sawn
grief
new-minted
sorrows
varnished
now broken-backed
boards rotted
the seat
caved in
though the arms
are still upright
and your copper
name-plaque
etched eternally bright
in weathered
lettering

crunch of
dusty gravel
and the camber
of dried grasses
we bear it
away
with the thought
of bearing
your remains
nine years
on

Over Brdo
Žrnovo
September 2010

My talisman

lemon-slice
tilted
lunar midday
skull-cap
or cuticle

reminding me
of the blue halfmoons
of your dying
nails
or
Celan's ever-yet
of poetry's facing
vapour trail
chalked across
the blue void

Alone at the door
Žrnovo house
September 2010

Up

in the morning gloaming
already gone
to the first life
gulls flocking
down to the icy cobbles
and barred windows
of Ship Street Great
for the first time
I met the *madeleine*
and spoke
with a baker
of poets
Duffy Larkin
Carlos Williams and Carver
trace elements
of our art

and knew again
for the nth time
life
is here
to live
to the last
in remembrance
and aftermath

Remembering Proust
Gibbon's Café, Dublin
4 December 2010

"She sent out for one of those short, plump little cakes called *petites madeleines*, which look as though they had been moulded in the fluted scallop of a pilgrim's shell. And soon, mechanically, weary after a dull day with the prospect of a depressing morrow, I raised to my lips a spoonful of the tea in which I had soaked a morsel of the cake. No sooner had the warm liquid, and the crumbs with it, touched my palate than a shudder ran through my whole body, and I stopped, intent upon the extraordinary changes that were taking place ... at once the vicissitudes of life had become indifferent to me, its disasters innocuous, its brevity illusory ..." *Swann's Way* (Marcel Proust, 1913).

Moon

in the cloud
do you see it
too
earthling
in this
life only

Belfast and Glasgow
9 December 2010

The window

at gloaming
my favourite
winter place
M's photo
next to
me

Belfast and Glasgow
9 December 2010

2011

"… I strike the board
it answers me
yes — yes
no — no …"

Zbigniew Herbert
from "A Knocker"

Between

Belfast and Glasgow
the gift got lost
briefly
or darkly
only to be resurrected
by the kind
chamber
of your voice

Belfast
8 January 2011

At the corner

of Gordon
and Hope
where we bid
goodbye
in wintry night
I find
at last
the hope denied
and so see
a
better version
of the present life

Leaving Glasgow
11 January 2011

The Sarajevo

heart-pin
given by one
who knew
the killing
hurt
of the living
now dead
but now
with one
who helps
to heal it
with a living
love

Miriam's birthday
12 January 2011

And as

Camus said
of one existence
out of Africa
in the midst
of winter
I finally learned
there was
in me
an invincible
summer

On the new life
Belfast
13 January 2011

It descended

from
a grandmother
in fearsome Germany
the green
jade elephant
with a delicate
link
sealing
the auspiciousness
of love

An old gift
Glasgow
21 March 2011

Dawn light

in the pastel
blue nautilus
of the shower
spangled
with droplets
like beauty
or
tears
running down
a child's enchanted
pane

Glasgow
22 March 2011

I lost

the scarf
for half
a day
and the young
Italian girl
who brought it down
the stairs
and back
like a lost child
was
for a second
the pinprick-presence
of Venus
herself

After the fear
Belfast café
29 March 2011

Birdsong

trilling again
in the morning
dusk
some fragrance
caught
on the air
but
not the rosescent
of Saint Therese
though
I think
I thought so
once
hoping
against hope

Love without hope
Belfast before Glasgow
31 March 2011

This time

late afternoon
after rains
and a call
on the second life
the wan sun
breaking open
like the heart
the perfect birches
svelte
and sylph-like
J at my shoulder
not a word
spoken
as we turn
toward the daffodils
and that
glorious bloom
the first
unrepeatable scent
imagined
a whole year
now
real
as this
incontrovertible silence

Miriam's deathday
4 April 2011

In the dream

you
were running
along a road
through fields
of golden orient
wheat
to meet me
before
the grief
might get to me

"Adam awoken found his dream"(Keats)
In flight over the Irish Sea
11 April 2011

Against

a sandstone spire
in Glasgow
late light
filling West Nile Street
with a dazzling
sun-shower
for
the winter was
survived
the spring here
in blossom
and a new
life
always evolving

To Glasgow Airport
11 April 2011

In the Arabic

café
on the question
of glosses
Rusmir says
we should not wish
to place
the text
in the shadow
of our egotism

In the Baščaršija
Sarajevo
23 April 2011

In daylight

I already
feel
the silence
of departure
like
last night's
dark sea
flecked
with memory's
lights

Before departure
Dubrovnik
26 April 2011

What gift

is this
what gift-giver
that came
so late
to me

Glasgow Airport
9 May 2011

One day

I will
have to say
out of our dying
or our living
goodbye
to
a second face
I loved
beyond
all others

Departing Glasgow
9 May 2011

Late light

cast on the Radisson
in the pastel sky
in the one place
in the one life
in the one world
in the one
solitude

After the gym
Belfast
12 May 2011

After

ten years
seventeen weeks
and two days
I thought
maybe
I was back
to the new lush
garden
thick with grasses
buttercup and clover
where the spangled
branch
of apocalypse
first fell

In garden sunshine
Belfast
14 July 2011

The day moon

like a moth
in bright daylight
or
a cabbage white
fluttering
up
in the morning dusk's
fading
night

Dusk in the maquis
Korčula
August 2011

Finally

it came
the flutter-flash
from the fig
to the laurel
when over
morning coffee
the golden oriole
unburdened me
of the fear
of the pain
that is always in
new life

Žrnovo garden
August 2011

How did

we
lose her
that Saturday
afternoon
when
everything changed

Belfast
Autumn 2011

Dear Angus

old ghost
it has taken
me
three years
and a new life
to feel
the full force
of your death
in the middle
of nowhere
in October
in Scotland

Remembering Angus Calder
Newtown Stewart
Dumfries and Galloway
2 October 2011

The woodsmoke

smell
wafting in
through the casements
like the tang
of destruction
itself
though somehow sweet
and beautiful
in the order
of my autumn things

Žrnovo house
12 October 2011

Tangerine cirrus

lit brilliantly at last light
on the late blue
though the hill
so dark
like existence
whose witness
I am
in the inner
firefight

Thinking of the fear
Žrnovo house
12 October 2011

The chestnuts

still
in the Monument's
pool
like the hard
bitter terrible pills
of their
undissolved deaths

Sarajevo children's monument
22 October 2011

The last morning

after
the last night
the crescent moon
like Islam's
slender cusp
by a lobe of dark
waxing
towards plenitude
in our new lives

Departures
Sarajevo Airport
24 October 2011

After

a long time
life
was good
you
were good
we
were good
this is how
it could be
this is how
it will be
and just now
the foggy Sarajevo hills
fall away
like something I had to let go
within me

Leaving Sarajevo on the early train
24 October 2011

The jewelled

circuit-board
of Glasgow
spreading out
like a shoal
of phosphorescence
the aisle and the seats
like an Odyssean galley
homing for
the true
antiquity of love

Belfast-Glasgow
Autumn 2011

There

is
only
always
the
one
moment

A line from an email
Belfast
December 2011

2012

"Take it that you have died today,
and that your life's story is ended;
and henceforward regard what further time
may be given you as an uncovenanted surplus ..."

Marcus Aurelius

Old Yiddish

proverb
there is no
competition between souls
but perhaps
no union either
we are ships passing
in a cosmic
question

Belfast
February 2012

Twelve

opened blossoms
on your little
tulip-tree
so delicate
and pale
the blush
at the base
of each
like the eleven
long years
since the last
breath
of your death
with one
more
now to come

Belfast garden
27 March 2012

I left

the door ajar
for easy
re-entry
then walked
to the place
in the year's
first warmth
the old birdsong
and budding
across the Lethe
of Ravenhill Road
daffodils
like a resurrection's
trumpets
the little bike
that might be hers
to the heavenly
scent
in sunshine
against a brilliant blue

but someone
was watching
from daily life
so I quickly
picked
two boughs
and stood
before the space
of the bush
alight with busybees
after
the red admiral
of your life
flew off
from a single
blossom
still unbruised
with brown
by its time's
short span

Walking to Bethlehem Nursery
Belfast
27 March 2012

The story

goes
that at
the height
of the whirlwind
Chinese generals
played
a game of grasshoppers
in their gilded cages

Driving
Belfast
27 March 2012

Three candles

in the sand
of a stand
the heavenly
iconostasis
far above
nothing compared
to this plain scene
of lit souls
in reality's earth
of raked circumference
one thicker and lower
another higher
and thinner
but yours
straight as a sapling
with its whole
life ahead

After the Requiem
Orthodox church
Dubrovnik
16 April 2012

Down

to two
already
yours
shorter and earth-bound
but the Other
waning too

One hour later
Orthodox church
Dubrovnik
16 April 2012

We gave

him life
and he became
and is
still becoming

we gave
her life
and she became
and is still
becoming
with us

Sarajevo
October 2011 – April 2012

I was afraid

of the cuts
we made
to the almond
the day before
because it is easier to live
in the old growth
of dead shade
than face
the heartwood's
fresh crosscuts
and cleared spaces
of new vistas
like a moth
still stuck
in the shadows
of a dawn
window

Dawn
Žrnovo
2 May 2012

Today

the third of May
a Thursday
a hot
clear day
I reconciled
my self
to some things
outwith
and within
in my destiny
for
as the poet says

Renovations
Žrnovo house
3 May 2012

I approached

the mirror
in the old storeroom
that hung
undisturbed
for fifty or so years
at least
and saw
in the faded
reflection-substance
my own face
arrived
already
in the land of ghosts
in the dust-coated
attic
above

Renovations
Žrnovo house
5 May 2012

On the pilgrim plane

God
is literally
finishing off
the last
true believers
irony
of ironies
or maybe
for one
who is sick and sorrowful
holy
of holies
anyway
I feel the mystery
at the heart of it
the whole
aging process
that unites
us all

Mounting a flight
Dubrovnik
6 May 2012

Instant idea

for
a poem
the hare
lying dying
a few minutes
before
in the grass
form of its death
Jake standing
staring
that terrible year
outwith
it all

On the train
Edinburgh-Glasgow
30 May 2012

Look how

it gets us
old age
the old
Irish poet
teeth rotten
with fags
sow's ear
in a silk tie
rumpled pretence of tweeds
condescending to everything
not him
or not in
the Irish case
or copula
did he ever
really love
does he ever
really enjoy
free of writing
grinding the bone meal or Burnhouse
of life
into *yes*
great poetry

Belfast
July 2012

I laid

a golden nail
on the enamel
sink
then fumbled
its lifting
and watched
it vanish
down the maw
of the drain
like the omen
it was
without illumination

In the house
31 July 2012

As if a full-stop

clarified
the whole sentence
backwards
with a brilliant
clarification
of vanishing
breath

Hearing of a death
7 August 2012

Poor Nano

not much
of a worker
a bit
of a fuck-up
what with
the drugs
yet it was he
who planted the tomato-patch
giving it
halfhearted attention
like so much
in life
where later
early one august morn
I would take
a photo
of Miriam
holding her bowl of tomatoes
that even still
holds her still life
on the hall wall
above
the vanished scene

On the terrace
Žrnovo
7-8 August 2012

The strange thing

is that
Death
is always
the same thing
happening
whenever
it happens

Žrnovo
8-9 August 2012

I forgot

for the first time
to go to the bench
where the past opens
to the present
continuous
the human
heart alone
discerns

Žrnovo
10 August 2012

I looked back

three times
the first two
willingly
seeing a corner
of the bench in maquis
the third
unwillingly
and so
seeing nothing
trying
to learn
to thole it
without looking back
like Peter
who denied
three times
before the cock crowed
or Lot
me reading the myth
who turned to stone
after his sudden loss

Leaving the bench
Žrnovo
16 September 2012

I remember

I remember
the day the kids
played
Germans and Partisans
in the old waterhole
bunker
boards now rotted
two sprouted saplings
Miriam hither and thither
on reconnoitre
stopped in her tracks
shouting warnings
of the coming danger
to her brother
like the neighbour's parrot
who haunts me still
with her mimicked voice
crying *Ja-cup Ja-cup*
as if still wandering the world
of the dead
seeking the beloved brothertime
and the love
they had

At the terrace table
Žrnovo
17 September 2012

A golden nail

of the same kind
suddenly appeared
on the rough board floor
catching a glint
in memory's
morning sun

Waking alone
Žrnovo
4-17 September 2012

The crescent moon

and morning star
clear over
antennae and chimneys
the lit windows
of close hallways
the big birch windy
and some other
pinprick of hope
strung spangling
to the acute angle
of planets and tenement
a vent's steam
the building's
human breath
in the blue first light
rising
to a first day
in the promised land

Fotheringay Road
Glasgow
Autumn 2012

And then we die

after all
the memory
and love
and suffering
still
no closer
to the whys and wherefores
of it
all

Belfast
Autumn 2012

2013

"… Mr Cogito
will be counted
among the species *minores*

he will receive indifferently
the verdict of men of letters

he employed the imagination
for wholly different purposes

he wanted to make of it
an instrument of compassion …"

Zbigniew Herbert
from "Mr Cogito and the Imagination"

Solo

in
the Emperor's Mosque
he stands and prays
bows and stands
in a hood
black as Death
before the lit Arabic
of white windows
Stars-of-David
and universal circles
to a Seljuk *mihrab*
the dome
of the void
filled with some subtle
exquisite scent
reminding me
of Miriam's
always
delicate presence

The Bistrik district
Sarajevo
February 2013

134

There it is

splendiferous London
lit bridges
girded over
the serpentine Thames
jewelled honeycomb
of hope
and joys and love
misery and power
this century's
high plateau
vulnerable before
the plagues and epidemics
that will surely come

Flight from Vienna
16 February 2013

One Saturday afternoon

at the threadbare hour
I swerved
from the broad way
and passed
her hospital window
in the orbital wing
where life still shone
on her final life
now gone as
Off Sales at The Oak Bar
and got upset
for the eleventh
commandment is
honour your dead
so noticing
thence
a new broad vista
I had never noticed

Off the Falls
Belfast
23 February 2013

Look

the primroses
you planted
that Saturday morning
still blooming
after twelve years
and a hard March
a bulb of seed
the robin
four or five tits
in the new day
outwith
the within
still
without

Belfast
31 March 2013

Nothing exists

without the other
no male
without female
no night
without day
no faith
without doubt
no life
without time
or was it
is it
vice versa

Belfast
Spring 2013

I'm back

to the place
I've really
never left
still wearing too-
worn clothes
thanks
to no shopping
my faithful shoes
like the Brecht poem
and a worn heart
to boot
wondering if
the school-gates are closed
to the eschatological return

The pressures

won't stop me going
for a moment
into the helium glow
to the one pure
moment of
the loss
of you

My mood

this day of days
in and out
like cloudy sunshine
now brightening
now darkening
in the living-room
where on the sofa
we half-learnt
the first alphabet
of your life
in abortive chrysalis
aborted
by "God"

Twelve years

to the minute
eleven forty-one
you left our light
our still-continuing
city

It's clear

the universe is
so complex and vast
that "probably" it has
no "origin" or "end"
no "meaning"
bound to the human space
and its little
"time-capsule"
words

Junk post

the gargoyle head
the wintry woody blue
skyline of New England
birdsong as always
and greenery
thwarted this year
by cold
and indeed
one gate closed
but the Other
open
walking in Hopper-light
my shadow to the left

daffodils full and bright
but your bush
in furry bud
like rabbit's paws
one only
in incipient bloom
after this hard-bitten
bitter winter
a lovely relief
I should
come again
and that again
something
was given

And so the new text read

Remember
your lovely sister

Love

4 April 2013
Miriam's deathday
Belfast

How similar

I have become
to my grandmother
sitting alone
with a mug of coffee
sitting with Bill
full of bereavement
I never noticed
or knew to name

Glasgow
14 April 2013

I remember those days

in The Hague
moving through the Mauritshuis
with its stanzas
of Vermeer-space
suggesting the sense
of love thwarted
or endangered
but enduring
during
the Dutch Wars

then taking
the tramlines
straight and shining
over grassy sleepers
in lush May
through Scheveningen's woods
to *World Forum Noord*
and the Tribunal's
Dantesque circles
at *Churchillplein*

Blown along

the bike-track
drifts of fluttering
heart-shaped beige catkins
like legions
of the lost
thronging

and imploring
the gates
of the living
Tribunal

And so up until now
the only always
here-and-now
Miriam and the Moses basket
the art
of Pharaoh's daughter
in the poet's eye
out of the coeval I
pushing forth love's basket
of bulrush and bitumen

from receding planes
into
the past presence
of the invisible foreground
of receiving *us*

"Lady Writing a Letter with Her Maid"
Vermeer
The Royal Picture Gallery
The Hague
2013

Still there

after a hard weather
the bloom
amid full leaf
the daffodils
almost gone
and though
muted
sad as ever
as my
steps recede

Belfast
15 May 2013

The small moment

extremely beautiful
like the magpie
in the ancient birch
flitting down
in sunshine and lightgreen
to another waving bough
like a thought inwith
its swaying whole

Fotheringay Road
Glasgow
May 2013

I love him

so much
especially
right now
when I see
in his lanky dreamy
gait a touch lost
and shy-sad
my father
when I first
knew him
as a little boy

After renting a flat
Connolly Station, Dublin
31 May 2013

Dreaming

Ellistron
dark
river vowels
glistening at five
in the afternoon

Written in sleep
Dreaming a place where Miriam was
3 June 2013

The extreme

artistry
of dreams
unrolling
from some spool
or rubric
not knowing
the end
at the beginning
the whole flow
deeply aslant

for the Ancients
had a point
in divining
otherworldly origins
in their preternatural
images

Belfast-Glasgow
June 2013

Under INRI

a candle lit
in memory of Miriam
in an old wood-panelled church
in Antwerpen
let us hope
against hope
at least
it shines
somehow
some place
we can never comprehend

Antwerp
7 June 2013

It appears

in many guises
and places
the extreme beauty of
the moon
like in sea-phosphorescence
of silver plate
filled from a Full one
that first time
on the watertaxi
ploughing the light

or tonight
seventeen years on
from the ferry
a sliver of crescent
of dark-honeyed amber
setting into dark headland
like a bookend
to all that time
past
in between
in the second life
of the mind's amber

12-15 June 2013
Korčula

Milky Way

above the weathervane's hunter
chimney breast of the cookhouse
at the corner of the terrace
overhanging
upside down
infinite space
the lack
of absolute darkness
inlaid with ingots
or with washes
of Magellanic Cloud
Belmont and/or Escher

for light only
is always
its bending mate
and splendid helpmeet

Korčula
12-19 June 2013

Above the others

her long lithe candle
new-planted
in the heartspace
of the gravel clockface
burns through another
June day
in the Orthodox church
in Dubrovnik
until from a choir's wall-chair
looking away
for a moment
five of the dead
had vanished
though strangely
I didn't see
the verger
do it
or any other
passing stranger

Dubrovnik
19 June 2013

I watched the bats

tumbling
and the morning star
maybe
over a garden
in The Hague
one house lit
in hope
the tree's top
shifting and swaying
ebbing and rising
ducking and feinting
like one night's sorrows
without catharsis
remedy or acquittal
in the natural history
of feeling's destruction

After the war crimes tribunals
The Hague
17 July 2013

I was eating

my fruit salad
sadly
half a stone's throw
from the new almond
where you held
once
the tomatoes
maybe
in the same
blue-and-white
bowl

On the terrace
Žrnovo
3 August 2013

Every day

your bench faces
the new light
at dawn
its red orb
over mountains
spilling
its liquid foil
into
the narrow channel
below
us
up early
to remember

Over Brdo
Žrnovo
11 August 2013

It was beautiful

in the dawn
sitting next to you
and the old scents
of New Hampshire
before the long trek
back to the hard world
hardened
by life

Over Brdo
Žrnovo
11 August 2013

Behind us

at the end
of a rough road
the bars of the bench
shine
like a smile
in the life
of the wild grasses
left behind

Turning towards Brdo
Žrnovo
11 August 2013

Totemic Dalmatian creature

the snail
a soft tongue
in a hard shell
whorled with mahogany and olive
flecked with blacks
a small immigrant
after rains
in this thirsty land
ingrained with ethnicities

In the polje
Žrnovo
11 August 2013

UNFINISHED FRAGMENTS
FINISHED

Watching

the trains
overlooking
Station East

Glasgow
July – September 2011

I love

going
in the morning
dusk

Belfast
2011

The nightingales

and the stars
singing ensemble
one chill night
whose Spartan poem
I forgot
to write

Žrnovo
2012 – 2013

The fresh

august
morning
a new day
given
but better yet
a new start

Žrnovo
2012 – 2013

A slash

of contrail
over the sunset sky
mesas of cloud
orange-lit
on the cobalt darkling
the comet-head shining
the tail trailing
into the non-wake
of time

Evening sorrow
Žrnovo
15 September 2013

For the first time

since the night before
Miriam's death
when I begged
for her life
in a corridor chair
I prayed at the pillow
to the unhearing yahweh-god
who only always
lets us down
then later
cupped my hands
more comfortably
at the Dubrovnik fountain
to the same allah
forgetting altogether
the wounded one
sombre as hell

that love
not be taken
from me
once again

In transit
Yom Kippur
13 September 2013

This time

anyway
I travelled light
without
the heart
of life
into munificent
September magnificence

First morning
Žrnovo
14 September 2013

The world welcomes

me back
warm sun
on my brow
like an old friend
at the open casement
swung open
to the eternal blue
where once
I saw and suffered
in the night coolth
true apocalypse
next to
the same almond
below
now stumped and weathered
in the black earth
wetted and fresh
with the tears
of night rain

Early morning
Žrnovo
14 September 2013

I can see

the sadness
in your back
says a friend
watching me watch
the sea-vistas
arms on the stone
of a mole
strange how
a back can speak

On the Lumbarda mole
15 September 2013

Burnt-wood-smell

on the beach
in September
all so clear and pure
the light-ripples
rippling
the sand-ripples
like a new love
after
we named
a beach in honour of you

Afternoon
Lumbarda mole
14 September 2013

They're falling

suddenly
those leaves
of autumn
a golden shoal
as if at the wind's behest
letting go
in one day's go
going deeper
into downwards time
the street ahead
and the road behind
an alley of leafmeal
lying

Thinking of Hopkins
("Spring and Fall: To a Young Child")
North Parade, Belfast
27 September 2013

2014

"I felt at home, strangely, because it is a miniature world. [...] One manor house, one farmhouse. A vineyard, a field of potatoes, a field of wheat, a cherry tree, an orchard. It has one of everything, so it is in a sense an ark. It is like large-scale things. Not in architecture or evolutionary leaps. I think it's an aberration. This notion of something that is small and self-contained is for me a moral and aesthetic ideal."

W.G. Sebald
from *A Place in the Country*

MacAdam

Memorials
on the *Falls*
that old word-wound
the headstone
and the heart-stone
and the Celtic cross
are polished blanks
as if waiting
for my own death
near your death-window
near your deathbed
this bleak midday
of bitter-biting
Irish rains
storminess ruffling
the limpidity
of pavement puddles
like the sand-pools
of those Donegal beach days
before it all came unstuck
when the coffee cup
and newspaper
were left
forever
in the hospital café
I had just passed

Falls Road, Belfast
25 January – 5 February 2014

Yellow cat's-cradles

of the old gantries
in the dawn's
sulphury blue
a twinkling easyjet
preparing to land
behind a row of poplars
silhouetted
as if a besom-broom
blown out of the East
from the Ukrainian drama
where history has
hardly ended

And Davos
be aware
and be apprised
with your Faustus
of capital
running amok
and wreaking
its havoc
the mass
ethicalized
here too
may yet arise
like a Luther or Brecht
to defenestrate
banksters and oligarchs
in a collective

catharsis
to roll the tumbril
for your shameless
self-indulgences

says at least
this easy passenger

Belfast-Glasgow
22-25 February 2014

Beautiful primrose

still so delicate
after all
this time
the last one planted
on your sickday
the first one up
in sunny February
on a mossy bed
under the privet hedge
atwinkle with waterlight
between two petals
in its bowl of being

for though
outwith
you're dead
you still exist
for me
like that glint of light
inwith
my innermost place

Belfast garden
26 February – 8 March 2014

The *M* of blossoms

in a floral wreath
on the grass
under the magnolia
made from camellia blooms
check-by-jowl
to the bay window
on whose sill
still lie
the paper letters
in a pot
near the sofa
where we played
first letters
which we mostly knew

this night
I remember the night
I stayed up
all night
by your bedside
till I took
a break
from the vigil
for coffee and a newspaper
then suddenly
called back
to the corridor
fell into the deepest

plexus-pit
of love's total fear
never
to return
to that stilled
coffee-cup

The Belfast house
3-23 April 2014

The birdsong

goes
on and on
a wash of daffodil
willow and eucalyptus
and that divine scent
at twenty yards
that hits me
yet again
before the pulsing thorax
of a honeybee
nestling on nectar
in a white chalice

The memorial magnolia
Miriam's deathday
4-23 April 2014

I found a snail

crossing the sidewalk
like the ones
in Dalmatia
yellowy-greeny
whorled
with bands of dark brown
heading for
its nirvana of hedge
and so saved it
of course
from its dangerous course
the way I failed
to save you
that cloudy-clement
breezy-bright
March day
when we went
AWOL on the towpath
unalert to alertness
and your final course
was settled

Morning
Miriam's deathday
Cross Parade, Belfast
4-23 April 2014

Not like

today
with the rain
that day
I had to swerve
from the daily mall
to Foster Green
and the wire bead-maze
pre-apocalypse

this swish of the wipers
on a windshield
raindropped with droplets
like tears fusing
the real life
the other life
the afterlife

cleared always
for the present pane only
in a blink of an eye

Forestside
Belfast
1-9 August 2014

In the darkroom

of this comparative dark
a luminous thing
is stirring still
and always
in the so-called "subconscious"
on the blank paper
in the first tray
a congealed image
is consciousness
materializing
being
though not yet
fixed and finished
till the fixer
in the next tray makes
momentary and executory
a new compound
free-floating
from its elements
ready to be
processed for centuries
inwith
the life of the language
that is
nothing less than
the life of language

Fotheringay Road
Glasgow
16 August 2014

So many

great times together
like this one
when small
with me
trying
to net the silvery fry
dispelling
our feints and dips
off the rocky mole
with its beacon's red lamppost

if it's really real
you can remember it
in the wake of a summer
again
I imagine
him giving a wave
a red T-shirt astern
in a water taxi
a dot
on the horizon of time

Jacob leaving, early morning
Korčula
5 September 2014

As always

forests and a railway
marshland and a marches
the crossing over sleepers
stretching
to a vanishing point
took us
past a huge brown slug
on a rainy walkway
to the spartan exhibition
knife axe mallet
documents and decrees
belongings and voices
to a little cubicle
to a child's jotter
still
practising handwriting
to the heart of things
in a loveless universe
to where
love is
the real
meaning or mover of everything

Mama i tata
me vole.
Mile voli tatu i mamu.

though now (or then)
only
supervised
in caring hope
by an older child
soon killed

Jasenovac, on the Sava
2-16 September 2014

The morning moon

a dome of a jellyfish
a lemon slice
helmet as broken
host
a *plis* or half-shell
a ghost
of the nocturnal light

After Jasenovac
Mid-September 2014

After a big storm

on the "knoll of the bear"
a windfall of apples
down in
a small garden
thick as moments
in a lifetime's
memory box
fallen near
fruited from
the trunk of consciousness

In the Zagreb hills
1-17 September 2014

The big black

evil bible
from her desk
opened
ominous title page
in eyeshot of
the tome of victims
promulgated in '41
the Aryan laws
the banning of Cyrillic
all "insults to Croatian honour"
in black and white
shelved for forty years or more
at a high school in Imoski
like a toxic germ
the holy writ
the simple text
a thriving slaughter
needs must
to breathe

Ustaše fonds
State Archives, Zagreb
September 2014
(During the IS Caliphate)

The old trail

actually
an antique road
thin long cobbles
lost in weeds
between gates and walls
through goatsheds
through centuries
a right-of-way
whose new value
in inherited awareness
cannot be reckoned
globally

Brdo shortcut
Žrnovo
15 September 2014

The parrot is gone

that once mimicked
Miriam's voice
who now
remembers it
but the eye
of a few hearts
by mischance
her life was quashed
like a morning snail
seeking the cool
dewy flagstones
of our verandah
once haunted
by the far parrot

Indian summer
Closing the house
Žrnovo
26-27 September 2014

A juvenile

praying mantis
or smaller species
pure green
from rains
I notice
by my boot
as I try to dislodge
a dead almond branch
from its high roost
its curved thorax
beaded with gold
filigree
its bug-eyes too
swaying in the breeze
like those other times
on the same land
I sat on a stonewall
for company
of your living memory
tireder now
our talisman
or touchstone
metempsychosis
before it vanishes
frighted
untouchable
into a ferny crevice

Žrnovo garden
22-25 September 2014

An ant

scurries across
the karst gravel
at one place
one moment
at another
the next
but both
the same
present
such
it seems to me
is eternity
right before
our very eyes

Žrnovo path
7-25 September 2014

Heaney's death

suggests to me
beguilingly
wisely
here on Miriam's bench
that a small life too
can finish
whole and rounded
even if
for both lives
the might-have-been
might have
been
still more
finished
round and whole

Above Žrnovo
September 2014

A space

but not a place
was promised
in a dream
that ran all night
in fitful images
of waiting
un-*claritas*
where no name
or time came
till
at the old five o'clock wake-up hour
of slow-burn pain
the rooster's republic
again clarified
uncovenanted surplus
of a Congo square
living free
"a dividend
from ourselves"
at the crowing dawn
and the blue sandbar
moon
that awaits
outwith

i.m. S.J.H.

Poem begun in sleep
Žrnovo house
September 2014

These whispering poems

snail-tracks
in the sun
dwelling for a time on gravel
an unravelling
skein of travelling
consciousness
friable as its earthed
lightening

Morning road
Žrnovo
September 2014

No headstone

through the rainy Irish nights
or cloudy empty
afternoons
but just
a small
Shaker box
of ashes
oval and swallow-tailed
rests still
with us
in the untouched
bedroom

Belfast
Late December 2014

2015

"... In order to revive the dead
and maintain the covenant

Mr Cogito's imagination
moves like a pendulum

it runs with great precision
from suffering to suffering

there is no place in it
for poetry's artificial fires

he wants to be true
to uncertain clarity ..."

Zbigniew Herbert
from "Mr Cogito and the Imagination"

A dramatic

dazzling
falling
of light
September or brilliant
evening
not quite
picked up
in the camera
the sun-
eclipse
in cloud
like an eggshell
of crescent
too subtle even
for the monitor
no sign
either
of the birdsong
silence

the word *eclipse*
bringing to mind
right
from the start
the day on Mljet
when Miriam was stung
by a bee

in a bag of grapes
and I killed it
out of undying love
in the brilliant shadowlands

Morning solar eclipse
Belfast
20 March 2015

That small flower

still there
up early
in late December
its fellows
long gone

Belfast garden
19 March 2015

Barred by a gate

we peer
through a grille
of distant
vista daubed
by the magnolia
between two buildings
as if locked out
from those harrowing days
the big beech behind
I never noticed
now overgrown
with a beard of ivy
almost till
the high airy branches
touching still
the sweet April
cloudy blue

until we turned
to watch
a car stopped
slowly
issuing
Sister Philip
this warm Easter Monday
who saw the events
and all the aftermath

as if that trope
on the road to Emmaus
the intense
coincidence suddenly
dawning

Near Bethlehem Nursery
6-7 April 2015

A quarter

of my life
with this
sorrow coming
back in time
fossilized
in a blink
only
the buried
life of living
feeling
relived

Čilipi
Outside Dubrovnik Airport
3-10 June 2015

Ants on karst

in streaming trails
back and forth
toing and froing
like us
busying themselves
with affairs
of hive and anthill
near sea-cliff and pine
a world
the glittering bay
one reach
of a uni-verse
each shadowy Aleppo
on the far high shore
a galaxy
or green supernova
the vague lie
of the always-next
reptilian island
a perpectival vastness
always and ever
impossible to ken

Pupnatska Luka
Korčula
6-10 June 2015

I lost it

yet again
the crimson scarf
totem or taboo
of time spent
with certain others
in
of all places
remote Knin
near the wild Lika

till returning
from retracing
my steps wending
through reconstructions
of a main thoroughfare
it was miraculously there
by a kiosk
in the midst of a junction
unnoticed and dusty
as Basho's road
from the deep south
as if vouchsafing
some purchase
on the happy
resurrection of time
once acknowledged
as life irrevocably lost

Dalmatia
12 April – 11 June 2015

IN THE MARCHES

That big tree

saw it all
a pine
now risen
way above
its juniors
of
I think
beech and ash
a spooky place
this April gloaming
the sheer pit-mouth karst
as yet undescended
by any speleologist
nor from which
not one child
Eurydice
was ever returned
by deepest love

In Jasenovac

the village
fluvial Middle
Europa
mouldering and dilapidated
riddled by two armies
its antiquities
of shed and shingle
derelict
one pockmarked building
bearing both
U for Ustaše
the Chetnik four *Ss*
in Cyrillic grid
storks came
as a real surprise
atop their ancestral nests
on lampposts or roof-trees
of pitched roofs
more loyal
than any irredentist
to the single
small place
along this road's grim tale

In Jasenovac

proper
the camp
Brickworks III
great broadleaf trees
rustling in ghost-breezes
saw also
all below
beside a river
next to tracks
a stone's throw
from marshes and deep woods
like past witnesses
in the face of a future
no individual mind
can now envisage

Remembering Jadovno & Jasenovac
Croatia
17-20 June 2015

His little legs

dangling
at the stooped crux
of a Turk's arms
someone had tied
his shoes that morning
he was ready
to go
with only love
he knew not where
now lost
to existence
even the shite *Sun*
saw *Life and Death*
the one who didn't make it
as we did
and still do
this day

Death of Alan Kurdi
Photographed near Bodrum, in the Aegean
3-5 September 2015

Germany

a new Jerusalem
born of defeat
and its East
astonishing Sebaldian swerve
along
a long-march motorway

whilst the old honoured word
Israel
is broken in two
into *Proper* and *Greater*
for the snail of the good
knows no borders

goes where it will
on the uncovenanted
single
terrace of history

"Time and patience bring the snail to Jerusalem,"
Proverb from the Irish
During the Syrian exodus
Belfast
3-5 September 2015

Two drops

on
two taps
perfect little orbs
reflecting
the world's light and shadow
all is hung
in the balance
before the quantum moment's
twofold drop of tension

Saturday morning alone
Belfast
5 September 2015

Ulrike Wirtz

whom I met
gallivanting in County Clare
near the Flaggy Shore
galloping behind her
into sea breakers misted
with crests like corn silk
before the lane back
from the rocks
between verges laden
with swished grass and cow parsley
to Harold's hostel
renovated by the host
and short-trousered veteran
who had seen
the Italian summer
at bloody Monte Cassino

and the *reprise*
under alpenglow
in the Hook
of borderland Germany
anti-Cruise '83
Einstein's station clock
at quaint Bischofswiesen
her chalet in woods
swift sex
on the snug's settle bed
before the night hike

to an overlook
over the lit village
fairy lights and *alpenmilk*
old enchantments
cowbells tinkling
in the downward dark

farewell then
at the door of the sanatorium
where she worked
Berlin to the bone
Alternativ in Red Wedding
now alone
in the Western boondocks
walking a wet mountain road
past roadside crucifixes
remarked upon with old inns
somewhere by Lawrence
down into evergreen
scenery backlit
again by alpenglow
sat near a stream
with my loss
suddenly dawning

then leaving
those two quatrains maybe
recording an indelible

moment on the balcony
typed up there
in faint indigo feint
hands on a railing
back to a field
radiant with goldenrod
hair a flowing Botticelli
rough-silky freedom
touch of Tartar
in the cheekbones
a smile's *soupçon*
our time's text
now buried deep
in some ancient file

before dropping
through the locked door
the key
to that supreme heart-flutter
maybe one life
is only ever
given a few

August — September 2015
Korčula

Three deer

at dusk
a doe
her fawns
stood-off and stock still
in headlights
in high forest
and three of us
a mother maybe
father and son
as if equals
at a distance
sharing
the magical moment
pausing us all
together
in strangeness

Near Krasno Polje
Croatia
14-27 September 2015

The sun

a day moon
in shifting
mountain cloud

just what you see
no flourishes

In the Velebit
Northern Croatia
16 September 2015

You popped out

in '93
smeared in purply vernix
wrinkled
and wise-looking
already like
our wee
dalai lama

now look at you
red-and-white Swiss cap
water polo T-shirt
army-green light trousers
and of course
alpine boots
trudging though
Bosnian fescue
in Velebit meadows
trekking the classic
karstic moonscape
vast sink-holes
greened by beechwoods
along knife-edge and sheer drop
its ancient striations
like the grooves of
the Žrnovo well
its weird mutated boulders
solitary South Sea statues

staring outwards
at the nothing
of sea-vistas
each step
a balancing act
on the limestone rocks

it somehow unpacks
something
some depth
here in the elemental
natural freedom
sorrow of my death
meeting Miriam's
imagine her here
and now
hiking the gorgeous heroic
Premužic trail
in the woods' clement September light
florilegium of sudden
brilliant alpines
imagining too
the last names and words
on my lips
for the loved ones

how life expands
with time
like time
the end of hiking
is itself

so
keep it real
with real realities

The Velebit Trek
17-27 September 2015

For the first time ever

just as I reached
my perfect solitary
terrace table coffee writing moment
I saw
a praying mantis flying
its wings spinning
in morning sunshine
towards the dewy-spangled grasses
between fig and oleander
as if a verification
of the primacy
of this present moment
well perceived

Žrnovo garden
18-23 November 2015

2016

"Is it not obvious that when through the modern media far things are brought near, the near things must be pushed far to make room for them? Imperceptibly, we become Lilliputians wandering in a Brobdingnag of our own contrivances and persuading ourselves that through contact with greatness we ourselves become greater. Then something happens to jerk us back to thoughts and people of our own size and significance. Most of the time when I was looking through that telescope, I was thinking not of the tremendous disasters that had befallen Leningrad and all Russia, but of the small stupidities, the acts of laziness or greed I had committed myself. Why had I not given the blue rug to Kolya's mother instead of leaving it behind by mistake? Why hadn't I sent Guzelimian his fishing rod?"

Hubert Butler
from "Peter's Window"

At last

it didn't
come up
the little yellow
primrose blossom
with rough tongue-like leaves
springing into
new light
in new life
like a comforting memory
or presence
where a robin prances
and I panic
with the old panic

perhaps because
it was a hard winter
in every sense
or because
time and tide covered
"the moments of agony"
with "currents of action"
or more to my liking
perhaps because
her ghost has been far
from me
these past days and months
the spring-willed life

symbol-and-spirit
was somehow
not sprung into spring

The Belfast garden
Mid-March 2016

The pyx

at Palm Sunday
the Eucharist
filtered through
exquisite Irish
pine-bough
on the pew before
even icons
and a choral harp
the last coccyx
of an old way
still vital
now that a remnant
minority
amongst others

but still
I refuse the offer of
Is mise aran na beatha
supreme copula
as adduced by Schillebeeckx
since like the host's single file
memory is most of life
my protest as *ant*
being
Unfair to Life
and to the fabulous
spring lamb riding
on a Jewish donkey

"I am the bread of life"
Palm Sunday, St Mary's Church
Belfast
20 March 2016

226

I left a coin

in a holy well
by Aodh's chapel
on Slieve League
on the way
to the pilgrim path
yours the brightest
a *50 Cents*
with that set of pillars
amongst four others
three dull
one brighter
in those wintry waters
under a cairn of stones

your tiny stone
deposited too
on a broad flag
atop
fitted rocks
and stacked slabs
facing its Irish sunshine
casting a shadow
these fifteen years
on

rooted to the spot
that old discipline
of the unrequited heart
I have to go
though

I want back already
I cannot stay
like once
I tried to stay
your coffin-lid
and got one last look
at your bloated unrecognizable face
before it left
forever

on a sea of rock
a stone boat
its prow
a phallic
standing stone
amidships
an ancient headstone
under
the unseen rudder
the hold barred
with your cold gold
I must trust

The Navigator
I have no monkish powers
to steer you home
to polestar or haven
a western isle
or Empty Zone

if such there be

Séipeal Aodh Mac Bricne
Sliabh Liag
Donegal
31 March — 14 April 2016

At a distance

in full beautiful blossom
for days
its sister
in the garden
four big blooms only
one bloom
for every year

but finally I went
a perfect spring day
to the coos of the woodpigeon
birdsong and the blue
a child's face in a car
a birch I had never noticed
the requisite magpie
hopping by
the daffodils faded
its brilliant mystical white
like memory itself
burst from furry pods
over fifteen years
of mossy earth
full of alighting bees
thon crow still
in the beech above
and nearby
the lightgreen buds
still
perfect as ever

Belfast – Korčula
May – June 2016

The poppies

are proliferating
in June
on the communal path
through our land
back towards
old Miko
and Austria-Hungary
on the map of the subtle hues
on the hall wall
the seven states
of his span
the eight wars
of a Balkan century

or forwards towards
the sea-dead
off Roman Libya
or the Aegean's
inflatable coracles
or corpses
heading
to the end
of the nation
state
in a new republic
of equal
lives

Ireland — Croatia
June — July 2016

The Heaney road

is now
not much
to look at
a weary declined
borderline crossroads
between Bellaghy
and Castledawson
the ancestral place
next "the tin hut"
an old remodelled pub
with a poet's corner
the road-worker stopped
for directions
with a tint of Scots
the scent of mown grass
outwith
the prison of death

but where
is
"the fairy road"
you took us on
so far inside
inwith your life

Between Bellaghy and Belfast
June – July 2016

We had

her real person
for just
two years
like the morning's
light-flooded lindens
on North Parade
before the afternoon's
darkening tempest
then
eternal night

Belfast
July 2016

I imagined Vojka

on Korčula
at sunrise
three days after
her death
and saw
"the afterlife"
as the preservation
of the past only
Miriam and Osman
and all the others
gone across
the whale road
to the dark land
somehow sharing
and somehow all aware
of the moments
when we had really loved

An epiphany, crossing Pelješac Channel
Early morning
24 August 2016

Beautiful exquisite

wan magenta
cyclamen
I dare not pluck
in pine needles
in a crevice of karst
umbered with goldish lichen
in quiet September
by the great lake
of Mljet
you have life too
I dare not end

On a bench
Mljet National Park
21 September 2016

What whitecaps

that day
of aftermath
on the way
to Dubrovnik
three days in
to the eschatological return
coursing the morning's
indigo sea
as if Yeatsian
white horses
at the Galway races

a forgotten poem
reminding me
much later
of the last day
of your penultimate September
at the dock
on the Lumbarda mole
from the high surf's rough-and-tumble
wondering with love
whether
as you always warned
you would last
another year
in time's
loving embrace

24 August – 27 September 2016
Dalmatia

Out

in the outback
on the summer's most far-off
September day
I found
a praying mantis
pure green
on a camber's chalky rut
which lying
seemed wounded
in the oozing thorax
grasping first
my index
then some plastic bits
in my khaki flap-pocket
maybe in
its last throes

so I nursed it
to no effect
when back
laid in a bowl
no doubt
you once used
jays in the almonds
on the blue sandbar sky
though
for a moment
or hour

it was like
miracle of miracles
Miriam back
with a barb
of thwarted tears
behind my eyes
its hurt green beauty
half-dead
like you in the hospital bed
my last vigil
at the September table

After the hike to Pupnat
26-28 September 2016

IN THE INTERIOR

What changes is us. *Life's frost*. In Bamiyam, lapis and dewless,
The Taliban are bombarding the great Buddhas of the interior.

March 2001

2017

"Only one thing remained reachable, close and secure amid all losses: language. Yes, language. In spite of everything, it remained secure against loss. But it had to go through its own lack of answers, through terrifying silence, through the thousand darknesses of murderous speech. It went through."

Paul Celan

FINIS